I'M LOVABLE!

KNOCK KNOCK®
VENICE, CALIFORNIA

Created, published, and distributed by Knock Knock
1635 Electric Ave.
Venice, CA 90291
knockknockstuff.com
Knock Knock is a registered trademark of Knock Knock LLC
Inner-Truth is a registered trademark of Knock Knock LLC

ISBN: 978-160106992-4
UPC: 825703-50153-7

10 9 8 7 6 5 4 3 2

FORGET THE
HOLY GRAIL. FORGET
THE FOUNTAIN OF YOUTH. FORGET WALDO.
What we're really seeking is proof that we're lovable. We want to be able to say, "I rock!" and really mean it. In short, we want to be Miss Piggy, who proclaimed, "I don't care what you think of me, unless you think I'm awesome. In which case you are right."

It's not that we want to be perfect. (Well, some of us do.) We want—and really need—to accept ourselves as we are: lovable, even with our flaws and idiosyncrasies. We need to stifle the inner (and outer) voices that tear us down and make us doubt.

The advice to love yourself and to be lovable didn't start with the self-help movement. It goes back much further. Ovid said it in *The Art of Love.* "Ut ameris, amabilis esto": "If you want to be loved, be lovable." Buddha said it too: "You yourself, as much as anybody in the entire universe, deserve your love and affection."

A little more recently, psychological research has backed up what our great thinkers knew: loving yourself is the key to happiness. Summarizing this research, the *New York Times* wrote, "giving ourselves a break and accepting our imperfections may be the first step toward better health. People who score high on tests of self-compassion have less depression and anxiety, and tend to be happier and more optimistic."

Such self-appreciation is a process, a practice. Whether you're almost there or you've got a long way to go, it all starts with being kind to yourself. Accept that who you are right now is good enough. It's the stuff you learned watching *Sesame Street*. Who on *Sesame Street* wasn't lovable? Even Oscar was lovable.

Researcher Fuschia Sirios noted in *Time* that the great thing about self-compassion is that it can be cultivated. And what better way to cultivate it than using a journal? With this journal you can record and process your quest for self-lovableness.

As noted self-help guru Deepak Chopra claims, "Journaling is one of the most powerful tools we have to transform our lives." And according to a widely cited study by James W. Pennebaker and Janel D. Seagal, "Writing about important personal experiences in an emotional way...brings about improvements in mental and physical health." Proven benefits include better stress management, strengthened immune systems, fewer doctor visits, and improvement in chronic illnesses such as asthma.

It's not entirely clear how journaling accomplishes all this. Catharsis is involved, but many also point to the value of organizing experiences into a cohesive narrative. According to *Newsweek*, some experts believe that journaling "forces us to transform the ruminations cluttering our minds into coherent stories." In many ways, journaling enables us to see the big picture, so we don't get lost in the small victories and defeats of any given day.

Specialists agree that in order to reap the benefits of journaling you have to stick with it, quasi-daily, for as little as five minutes at a time (at least fifteen minutes, however, is best), even on the days you feel totally in love with yourself. Finding regular writing times and comfortable locations can help with consistency. If you find yourself unable to think of a single lovable thing, don't stress. Instead, use the quotes inside this journal as a jumping-off point for observations and explorations.

Write whatever comes, and don't criticize it; journaling is a means of self-reflection, not a structured composition. In other words, spew. Finally, determine a home for your journal where you can find it when you're feeling self-critical; maybe keep it by the mirror.

Everyone is capable of finding, nurturing, and expressing the lovableness inside of them. Comedian Margaret Cho puts it quite eloquently: "I am so beautiful, sometimes people weep when they see me. And it has nothing to do with what I look like really, it is just that I gave myself the power to say that I am beautiful." Choose to love yourself and to be lovable and write about it here. If there are days you can't reach Cho's level of acceptance, quote self-help guru Stuart Smalley instead: "I'm good enough. I'm smart enough, and doggone it, people like me!"

To love oneself is the beginning of a lifelong romance.

Oscar Wilde

WHY I'M SO LOVABLE TODAY:

Empathy

Empathy is seeing with the eyes of another, listening with the ears of another & feeling with the heart of another Alfred Adler

You can only understand people if you feel them in yourself John Steinbeck

If you judge people, you have no time to love them Mother Teresa

HOW LOVABLE I CURRENTLY FEEL:

PTD

"Well, I am pretty," replied Charlotte. "There's no denying that. Almost all spiders are rather nice-looking. I'm not as flashy as some, but I'll do."

E. B. White

WHY I'M SO LOVABLE TODAY:

Sincerity

It is not so important to be serious as it is to be serious about the important things

If you would be loved, love and be lovable.

Benjamin Franklin

WHY I'M SO LOVABLE TODAY:

_____

_____

_____

_____

_____

_____

_____

_____

_____

_____

_____

_____

_____

_____

_____

_____

_____

_____

HOW LOVABLE I CURRENTLY FEEL:

Beauty is all about loving who you are. And if you have a problem with that, may I suggest you try loving who I am?

Miss Piggy

WHY I'M SO LOVABLE TODAY:

_____

_____

_____

_____

_____

_____

_____

_____

_____

_____

_____

_____

_____

_____

_____

_____

_____

_____

_____

HOW LOVABLE I CURRENTLY FEEL:

She was becoming herself and daily casting aside that fictitious self which we assume like a garment with which to appear before the world.

Kate Chopin

WHY I'M SO LOVABLE TODAY:

_____

_____

_____

_____

_____

_____

_____

_____

_____

_____

_____

_____

_____

_____

_____

_____

_____

HOW LOVABLE I CURRENTLY FEEL:

I am not pretty. I am not beautiful. I am as radiant as the sun.

Suzanne Collins

WHY I'M SO LOVABLE TODAY:

HOW LOVABLE I CURRENTLY FEEL:

The supreme happiness of life is the conviction that we are loved; loved for ourselves—say rather, loved in spite of ourselves.

Victor Hugo

WHY I'M SO LOVABLE TODAY:

_____

_____

_____

_____

_____

_____

_____

_____

_____

_____

_____

_____

_____

_____

_____

HOW LOVABLE I CURRENTLY FEEL:

To say
"I love you"
one must
know first
how to say
the "I."

Ayn Rand

WHY I'M SO LOVABLE TODAY:

_____

_____

_____

_____

_____

_____

_____

_____

_____

_____

_____

_____

_____

_____

_____

_____

_____

HOW LOVABLE I CURRENTLY FEEL:

Look at the sky: that is for you. Look at each person's face as you pass on the street: those faces are for you. And the street itself, and the ground under the street, and the ball of fire underneath the ground: all these things are for you.

Miranda July

DATE		

WHY I'M SO LOVABLE TODAY:

_____

_____

_____

_____

_____

_____

_____

_____

_____

_____

_____

_____

_____

_____

_____

_____

_____

HOW LOVABLE I CURRENTLY FEEL:

You cannot convince people to love you. This is an absolute rule. No one will ever give you love because you want him or her to give it.

Cheryl Strayed

WHY I'M SO LOVABLE TODAY:

_____

_____

_____

_____

_____

_____

_____

_____

_____

_____

_____

_____

_____

_____

_____

_____

_____

_____

HOW LOVABLE I CURRENTLY FEEL:

To be fully seen by somebody, then, and to be loved anyhow— this is a human offering that can border on the miraculous.

Elizabeth Gilbert

WHY I'M SO LOVABLE TODAY:

_____

_____

_____

_____

_____

_____

_____

_____

_____

_____

_____

_____

_____

_____

_____

_____

_____

HOW LOVABLE I CURRENTLY FEEL:

I can't deny the fact that you like me, right now, you like me!

Sally Field

DATE		

WHY I'M SO LOVABLE TODAY:

_____

_____

_____

_____

_____

_____

_____

_____

_____

_____

_____

_____

_____

_____

_____

_____

_____

_____

HOW LOVABLE I CURRENTLY FEEL:

I want to date myself, but I can't figure out how! You want to date me instead? You're so lucky!

Rick Riordan

WHY I'M SO LOVABLE TODAY:

_____

_____

_____

_____

_____

_____

_____

_____

_____

_____

_____

_____

_____

_____

_____

_____

_____

_____

HOW LOVABLE I CURRENTLY FEEL:

I've never felt like I needed to change. I've always thought, "If you want somebody different, pick somebody else."

Melissa McCarthy

DATE		

WHY I'M SO LOVABLE TODAY:

_____

_____

_____

_____

_____

_____

_____

_____

_____

_____

_____

_____

_____

_____

_____

_____

_____

HOW LOVABLE I CURRENTLY FEEL:

They say I have no hits and I'm difficult to work with, and they say that like it's a bad thing.

Tom Waits

WHY I'M SO LOVABLE TODAY:

_____

_____

_____

_____

_____

_____

_____

_____

_____

_____

_____

_____

_____

_____

_____

HOW LOVABLE I CURRENTLY FEEL:

I can have oodles of charm when I want to.

Kurt Vonnegut

WHY I'M SO LOVABLE TODAY:

_____

_____

_____

_____

_____

_____

_____

_____

_____

_____

_____

_____

_____

_____

_____

_____

_____

_____

HOW LOVABLE I CURRENTLY FEEL:

When I was around 18, I looked in the mirror and said, *You're either going to love yourself or hate yourself.* And I decided to love myself. That changed a lot of things.

Queen Latifah

WHY I'M SO LOVABLE TODAY:

_____

_____

_____

_____

_____

_____

_____

_____

_____

_____

_____

_____

_____

_____

_____

_____

HOW LOVABLE I CURRENTLY FEEL:

Bosom not as copious as she would wish, but has noticed that Botticelli bosoms are not big either. Legs OK, according to husband. Freckles.

Julia Child

	DATE	

WHY I'M SO LOVABLE TODAY:

_____

_____

_____

_____

_____

_____

_____

_____

_____

_____

_____

_____

_____

_____

_____

_____

_____

_____

HOW LOVABLE I CURRENTLY FEEL:

I celebrate myself.

Walt Whitman

WHY I'M SO LOVABLE TODAY:

_____

_____

_____

_____

_____

_____

_____

_____

_____

_____

_____

_____

_____

_____

_____

_____

_____

_____

HOW LOVABLE I CURRENTLY FEEL:

I think some people like me because I'm different. I don't think like everybody else.

Iris Apfel

WHY I'M SO LOVABLE TODAY:

_____

_____

_____

_____

_____

_____

_____

_____

_____

_____

_____

_____

_____

_____

_____

_____

_____

HOW LOVABLE I CURRENTLY FEEL:

The only childhood truly deserving of the title "privileged" is one which imbues someone with a capacity to be a friend to themselves.

Alain de Botton

DATE

WHY I'M SO LOVABLE TODAY:

_____

_____

_____

_____

_____

_____

_____

_____

_____

_____

_____

_____

_____

_____

_____

HOW LOVABLE I CURRENTLY FEEL:

I like to think that my arrogance, impetuosity, impatience, selfishness, and greed are the qualities that make me the lovable chap I am.

Richard Hammond

WHY I'M SO LOVABLE TODAY:

_____

_____

_____

_____

_____

_____

_____

_____

_____

_____

_____

_____

_____

_____

_____

HOW LOVABLE I CURRENTLY FEEL:

Very early in life, I realized that the most important relationship is the one you have with yourself. And if you figure that out, every other relationship is a plus, not a must.

Diane von Furstenberg

WHY I'M SO LOVABLE TODAY:

_____

_____

_____

_____

_____

_____

_____

_____

_____

_____

_____

_____

_____

_____

_____

_____

_____

_____

HOW LOVABLE I CURRENTLY FEEL:

Whenever I dwell for any length of time on my own shortcomings, they gradually begin to seem mild, harmless, rather engaging little things, not at all like the staring defects in other people's characters.

Margaret Halsey

WHY I'M SO LOVABLE TODAY:

HOW LOVABLE I CURRENTLY FEEL:

**Klutziness is endearing.
I like imperfection.**

Elizabeth Banks

WHY I'M SO LOVABLE TODAY:

_____

_____

_____

_____

_____

_____

_____

_____

_____

_____

_____

_____

_____

_____

_____

_____

HOW LOVABLE I CURRENTLY FEEL:

Some people are worth melting for.

Olaf (in *Frozen*)

WHY I'M SO LOVABLE TODAY:

_____

_____

_____

_____

_____

_____

_____

_____

_____

_____

_____

_____

_____

_____

_____

_____

_____

_____

_____

HOW LOVABLE I CURRENTLY FEEL:

I am so beautiful, sometimes people weep when they see me. And it has nothing to do with what I look like really, it is just that I gave myself the power to say that I am beautiful.

Margaret Cho

WHY I'M SO LOVABLE TODAY:

_____

_____

_____

_____

_____

_____

_____

_____

_____

_____

_____

_____

_____

_____

_____

_____

_____

_____

_____

HOW LOVABLE I CURRENTLY FEEL:

I was once afraid of people saying, "Who does she think she is?" Now I have the courage to stand and say, "This is who I am."

Oprah Winfrey

WHY I'M SO LOVABLE TODAY:

_____

_____

_____

_____

_____

_____

_____

_____

_____

_____

_____

_____

_____

_____

_____

_____

_____

HOW LOVABLE I CURRENTLY FEEL:

Charm is the ability to make someone else think that both of you are pretty wonderful.

Kathleen Winsor

WHY I'M SO LOVABLE TODAY:

_____

_____

_____

_____

_____

_____

_____

_____

_____

_____

_____

_____

_____

_____

_____

_____

_____

HOW LOVABLE I CURRENTLY FEEL:

My heart always leads me to me!

Stephen Colbert

WHY I'M SO LOVABLE TODAY:

_____

_____

_____

_____

_____

_____

_____

_____

_____

_____

_____

_____

_____

_____

_____

_____

HOW LOVABLE I CURRENTLY FEEL:

Delusions of grandeur make me feel a lot better about myself.

Jane Wagner

WHY I'M SO LOVABLE TODAY:

_____

_____

_____

_____

_____

_____

_____

_____

_____

_____

_____

_____

_____

_____

_____

_____

HOW LOVABLE I CURRENTLY FEEL:

If we go down into ourselves we find that we possess exactly what we desire.

Simone Weil

WHY I'M SO LOVABLE TODAY:

_____

_____

_____

_____

_____

_____

_____

_____

_____

_____

_____

_____

_____

_____

_____

_____

HOW LOVABLE I CURRENTLY FEEL:

It's always been inside of you, you, you /
And now it's time to let it through /
'Cause baby, you're a firework /
Come on show them what you're worth /
Make them go, "Oh, oh, oh" /
As you shoot across the sky.

Katy Perry

WHY I'M SO LOVABLE TODAY:

_____

_____

_____

_____

_____

_____

_____

_____

_____

_____

_____

_____

_____

_____

_____

_____

_____

_____

_____

HOW LOVABLE I CURRENTLY FEEL:

The externals are simply so many props; everything we need is within us.

Etty Hillesum

WHY I'M SO LOVABLE TODAY:

_____

_____

_____

_____

_____

_____

_____

_____

_____

_____

_____

_____

_____

_____

_____

_____

_____

_____

HOW LOVABLE I CURRENTLY FEEL:

What I cannot love, I overlook.

Anaïs Nin

WHY I'M SO LOVABLE TODAY:

_____

_____

_____

_____

_____

_____

_____

_____

_____

_____

_____

_____

_____

_____

_____

_____

_____

HOW LOVABLE I CURRENTLY FEEL:

Self-love, my liege, is not so vile a sin As self-neglecting.

William Shakespeare

WHY I'M SO LOVABLE TODAY:

_____

_____

_____

_____

_____

_____

_____

_____

_____

_____

_____

_____

_____

_____

_____

_____

_____

HOW LOVABLE I CURRENTLY FEEL:

About all you can do in life is be who you are. Some people will love you for you. Most will love you for what you can do for them, and some won't like you at all.

Rita Mae Browne

WHY I'M SO LOVABLE TODAY:

_____

_____

_____

_____

_____

_____

_____

_____

_____

_____

_____

_____

_____

_____

_____

_____

_____

HOW LOVABLE I CURRENTLY FEEL:

Do your thing and don't care if they like it.

Tina Fey

WHY I'M SO LOVABLE TODAY:

_____

_____

_____

_____

_____

_____

_____

_____

_____

_____

_____

_____

_____

_____

_____

_____

_____

HOW LOVABLE I CURRENTLY FEEL:

People are like stained-glass windows. They sparkle and shine when the sun is out, but when the darkness sets in, their true beauty is revealed only if there is light from within.

Elizabeth Kübler-Ross

DATE

WHY I'M SO LOVABLE TODAY:

_____

_____

_____

_____

_____

_____

_____

_____

_____

_____

_____

_____

_____

_____

_____

_____

_____

_____

HOW LOVABLE I CURRENTLY FEEL:

You your best thing.

Toni Morrison

WHY I'M SO LOVABLE TODAY:

_____

_____

_____

_____

_____

_____

_____

_____

_____

_____

_____

_____

_____

_____

_____

_____

_____

HOW LOVABLE I CURRENTLY FEEL:

I love that you get cold when it's 71 degrees out. I love that it takes you an hour and a half to order a sandwich. I love that you get a little crinkle above your nose when you're looking at me like I'm nuts.... And I love that you are the last person I want to talk to before I go to sleep at night.

Nora Ephron

DATE		

WHY I'M SO LOVABLE TODAY:

_____

_____

_____

_____

_____

_____

_____

_____

_____

_____

_____

_____

_____

_____

_____

_____

_____

_____

_____

_____

HOW LOVABLE I CURRENTLY FEEL:

Always be a first-rate version of yourself, instead of a second-rate version of somebody else.

Judy Garland

WHY I'M SO LOVABLE TODAY:

HOW LOVABLE I CURRENTLY FEEL:

When I see your face, there is not
a thing that I would change /
'Cause you're amazing, just
the way you are /
And when you smile, the whole
world stops and stares for a while.

Bruno Mars

WHY I'M SO LOVABLE TODAY:

_____

_____

_____

_____

_____

_____

_____

_____

_____

_____

_____

_____

_____

_____

_____

_____

_____

HOW LOVABLE I CURRENTLY FEEL:

I am not eccentric.
It's just that I am more
alive than most people.
I am an unpopular
electric eel set in a
pond of goldfish.

Edith Sitwell

WHY I'M SO LOVABLE TODAY:

_____

_____

_____

_____

_____

_____

_____

_____

_____

_____

_____

_____

_____

_____

_____

_____

_____

_____

HOW LOVABLE I CURRENTLY FEEL:

Forget your perfect
offering /
There is a crack in
everything /
That's how the light
gets in.

Leonard Cohen

WHY I'M SO LOVABLE TODAY:

_____

_____

_____

_____

_____

_____

_____

_____

_____

_____

_____

_____

_____

_____

_____

_____

_____

_____

HOW LOVABLE I CURRENTLY FEEL:

I think the healthy way to live is to make friends with the beast inside oneself... the shadow, the dark side of one's nature. Have fun with it. It's to accept everything about ourselves.

Anthony Hopkins

WHY I'M SO LOVABLE TODAY:

_____

_____

_____

_____

_____

_____

_____

_____

_____

_____

_____

_____

_____

_____

_____

_____

HOW LOVABLE I CURRENTLY FEEL:

The privilege of a lifetime
is being who you are.

Joseph Campbell

WHY I'M SO LOVABLE TODAY:

_____

_____

_____

_____

_____

_____

_____

_____

_____

_____

_____

_____

_____

_____

_____

_____

HOW LOVABLE I CURRENTLY FEEL:

When I lay my head
on the pillow at night
I can say I was a decent
person today. That's
when I feel beautiful.

Drew Barrymore

WHY I'M SO LOVABLE TODAY:

_____

_____

_____

_____

_____

_____

_____

_____

_____

_____

_____

_____

_____

_____

_____

_____

_____

HOW LOVABLE I CURRENTLY FEEL:

"You is kind," she say, "you is smart. You is important."

Kathryn Stockett

DATE		

WHY I'M SO LOVABLE TODAY:

_____

_____

_____

_____

_____

_____

_____

_____

_____

_____

_____

_____

_____

_____

_____

_____

_____

_____

HOW LOVABLE I CURRENTLY FEEL:

The moment you doubt
whether you can fly,
you cease forever to be
able to do it.

J. M. Barrie

WHY I'M SO LOVABLE TODAY:

_____

_____

_____

_____

_____

_____

_____

_____

_____

_____

_____

_____

_____

_____

_____

_____

_____

_____

HOW LOVABLE I CURRENTLY FEEL:

I think I'm lovable. That's the gift
God gave me. I don't do anything
to be lovable. I have no control.

Ann B. Davis

WHY I'M SO LOVABLE TODAY:

_____

_____

_____

_____

_____

_____

_____

_____

_____

_____

_____

_____

_____

_____

_____

_____

HOW LOVABLE I CURRENTLY FEEL:

Instead of looking in the mirror and focusing on your flaws, look in the mirror and appreciate your best features... everyone has them.

Demi Lovato

WHY I'M SO LOVABLE TODAY:

_____

_____

_____

_____

_____

_____

_____

_____

_____

_____

_____

_____

_____

_____

_____

_____

HOW LOVABLE I CURRENTLY FEEL:

It is sad to grow old but nice to ripen.

Brigitte Bardot

WHY I'M SO LOVABLE TODAY:

_____

_____

_____

_____

_____

_____

_____

_____

_____

_____

_____

_____

_____

_____

_____

_____

_____

HOW LOVABLE I CURRENTLY FEEL:

I seem slowly to be getting over what I imagined was the matter with me.

Robert Frost

WHY I'M SO LOVABLE TODAY:

_____

_____

_____

_____

_____

_____

_____

_____

_____

_____

_____

_____

_____

_____

_____

_____

_____

HOW LOVABLE I CURRENTLY FEEL:

A person's a person, no matter how small.

Dr. Seuss

WHY I'M SO LOVABLE TODAY:

_____

_____

_____

_____

_____

_____

_____

_____

_____

_____

_____

_____

_____

_____

_____

_____

HOW LOVABLE I CURRENTLY FEEL:

Sometimes the thing that's weird about you is the thing that's cool about you.

Maureen Dowd

WHY I'M SO LOVABLE TODAY:

_____

_____

_____

_____

_____

_____

_____

_____

_____

_____

_____

_____

_____

_____

_____

_____

_____

_____

_____

HOW LOVABLE I CURRENTLY FEEL:

So sensitive, said a family friend, that she could feel the grass grow under her feet.

Bill Roorbach

WHY I'M SO LOVABLE TODAY:

_____

_____

_____

_____

_____

_____

_____

_____

_____

_____

_____

_____

_____

_____

_____

_____

_____

_____

_____

HOW LOVABLE I CURRENTLY FEEL:

He saw in me more than I could see in myself. Whenever he peeled the image from the Polaroid negative, he would say, "With you I can't miss."

Patti Smith

WHY I'M SO LOVABLE TODAY:

_____

_____

_____

_____

_____

_____

_____

_____

_____

_____

_____

_____

_____

_____

_____

_____

_____

_____

HOW LOVABLE I CURRENTLY FEEL:

I remember looking in the mirror as a kid and, it would be like for an hour at a time, and I'd be like: "I'm just so beautiful. Everybody is so lucky that they get to look at me." And of course that changes as you get older, but I may have held on to that little-kid feeling that was me alone in my bathroom.

Lena Dunham

WHY I'M SO LOVABLE TODAY:

_____

_____

_____

_____

_____

_____

_____

_____

_____

_____

_____

_____

_____

_____

_____

_____

_____

HOW LOVABLE I CURRENTLY FEEL:

I never loved another
person the way I
loved myself.

Mae West

DATE		

WHY I'M SO LOVABLE TODAY:

_____

_____

_____

_____

_____

_____

_____

_____

_____

_____

_____

_____

_____

_____

_____

_____

_____

HOW LOVABLE I CURRENTLY FEEL:

Embrace who you are. Literally.
Hug yourself. Accept who you are.
Unless you're a serial killer.

Ellen DeGeneres

WHY I'M SO LOVABLE TODAY:

_____

_____

_____

_____

_____

_____

_____

_____

_____

_____

_____

_____

_____

_____

_____

_____

_____

_____

_____

_____

HOW LOVABLE I CURRENTLY FEEL:

You're all you've got.

Janis Joplin

WHY I'M SO LOVABLE TODAY:

_____

_____

_____

_____

_____

_____

_____

_____

_____

_____

_____

_____

_____

_____

_____

_____

_____

_____

HOW LOVABLE I CURRENTLY FEEL:

I feel pretty /
Oh, so pretty /
That the city should
    give me its key. /
A committee /
Should be organized
    to honor me.

Stephen Sondheim

WHY I'M SO LOVABLE TODAY:

_____

_____

_____

_____

_____

_____

_____

_____

_____

_____

_____

_____

_____

_____

_____

_____

_____

HOW LOVABLE I CURRENTLY FEEL:

I was sweaty, and my hair was matted and all over the place. And I was happy and hot and accomplishing a lot and running around, and I could feel my heart beating, and I felt beautiful.

Angelina Jolie

WHY I'M SO LOVABLE TODAY:

_____
_____
_____
_____
_____
_____
_____
_____
_____
_____
_____
_____
_____
_____
_____
_____
_____

HOW LOVABLE I CURRENTLY FEEL:

A man cannot be comfortable without *his own* approval.

Mark Twain

WHY I'M SO LOVABLE TODAY:

_____

_____

_____

_____

_____

_____

_____

_____

_____

_____

_____

_____

_____

_____

_____

_____

_____

HOW LOVABLE I CURRENTLY FEEL:

We are all
worms, but
I do believe
that I am a
glow-worm.

Winston Churchill

WHY I'M SO LOVABLE TODAY:

_____

_____

_____

_____

_____

_____

_____

_____

_____

_____

_____

_____

_____

_____

_____

_____

_____

_____

HOW LOVABLE I CURRENTLY FEEL:

When all else fails, you always have delusion.

Conan O'Brien

WHY I'M SO LOVABLE TODAY:

_____

_____

_____

_____

_____

_____

_____

_____

_____

_____

_____

_____

_____

_____

_____

_____

_____

_____

HOW LOVABLE I CURRENTLY FEEL:

Because I'm good enough,
I'm smart enough, and
doggone it, people like me!

Stuart Smalley

WHY I'M SO LOVABLE TODAY:

_____

_____

_____

_____

_____

_____

_____

_____

_____

_____

_____

_____

_____

_____

_____

_____

_____

_____

HOW LOVABLE I CURRENTLY FEEL:

The universe and the
light of the stars
come through me.
I am the crescent
moon put up over the
gate to the festival.

Rumi

WHY I'M SO LOVABLE TODAY:

_____

_____

_____

_____

_____

_____

_____

_____

_____

_____

_____

_____

_____

_____

_____

_____

HOW LOVABLE I CURRENTLY FEEL:

It was like the classic scene in the movies where one lover is on the train and one is on the platform and the train starts to pull away, and the lover on the platform begins to trot along and then jog and then sprint and then gives up altogether as the train speeds irrevocably off. Except in this case I was all the parts: I was the lover on the platform, I was the lover on the train. And I was also the train.

Lorrie Moore

WHY I'M SO LOVABLE TODAY:

_____

_____

_____

_____

_____

_____

_____

_____

_____

_____

_____

_____

_____

_____

_____

_____

HOW LOVABLE I CURRENTLY FEEL:

We begin to find and become
ourselves when we notice
how we are already found,
already truly, entirely,
wildly, messily, marvelously
who we were born to be.

Anne Lamott

WHY I'M SO LOVABLE TODAY:

___

HOW LOVABLE I CURRENTLY FEEL:

You have been criticizing yourself for years, and it hasn't worked. Try approving of yourself and see what happens.

Louise L. Hay

WHY I'M SO LOVABLE TODAY:

_____

_____

_____

_____

_____

_____

_____

_____

_____

_____

_____

_____

_____

_____

_____

_____

_____

_____

_____

HOW LOVABLE I CURRENTLY FEEL:

Does the river try to please a tree?
Does the bird try to please a stone?
In nature, things are simply who and
what they are. A tree trying to please
the river would be ridiculous....
What if I put all my energy and power
into being me instead of someone else's
version of me?

Paula D'Arcy

WHY I'M SO LOVABLE TODAY:

_____

_____

_____

_____

_____

_____

_____

_____

_____

_____

_____

_____

_____

_____

_____

_____

_____

_____

HOW LOVABLE I CURRENTLY FEEL:

Dare to love yourself as if you were a rainbow with gold at both ends.

Aberjhani

DATE		

WHY I'M SO LOVABLE TODAY:

_____

_____

_____

_____

_____

_____

_____

_____

_____

_____

_____

_____

_____

_____

_____

HOW LOVABLE I CURRENTLY FEEL:

The greatest thing
in the world is to
know how to belong
to oneself.

Michel de Montaigne

WHY I'M SO LOVABLE TODAY:

_____

_____

_____

_____

_____

_____

_____

_____

_____

_____

_____

_____

_____

_____

_____

_____

HOW LOVABLE I CURRENTLY FEEL:

Self-esteem isn't everything; it's just that there's nothing without it.

Gloria Steinem

WHY I'M SO LOVABLE TODAY:

_____

_____

_____

_____

_____

_____

_____

_____

_____

_____

_____

_____

_____

_____

_____

_____

_____

_____

_____

HOW LOVABLE I CURRENTLY FEEL:

You deserve love and you'll get it.

Amy Poehler

WHY I'M SO LOVABLE TODAY:

_____

_____

_____

_____

_____

_____

_____

_____

_____

_____

_____

_____

_____

_____

_____

_____

_____

_____

HOW LOVABLE I CURRENTLY FEEL:

xoxo.

Knock Knock